LONDON AFTER DARK

Destitute woman
Westminster

BOOKS BY GEOFFREY FLETCHER

GEOFFREY S. FLETCHER

LONDON
AFTER DARK

ARCO PUBLISHING COMPANY, INC., NEW YORK

First published in the United States
by Arco Publishing Company, Inc.
219 Park Avenue South, New York, N.Y. 10003

© Geoffrey S. Fletcher 1969

Printed in Great Britain

Contents

While London sleeps

And all the lamps are gleaming

Millions of its people now lie sweetly dreaming.

Some have no home to go

And o'er their sorrows weep,

Others laugh and play the game

While London's fast asleep.

A song my mother taught me, originally sung
by George Lashwood at the Holborn Empire

Gas lamp
Man in Moon
Passage
4 am
SSF   Regan St.

Introduction

Ah London! London! our delight,
Great flower that opens but at night,
Great City of the midnight sun,
Whose day begins when day is done.
                                 Richard Le Gallienne

'IN THE BIG CITY,' says O. Henry in *The Four Million*, 'the twin spirits Romance and Adventure are always abroad seeking worthy wooers. As we roam the streets they slyly peep at us and challenge us in twenty different guises. Without knowing why, we look up suddenly to see in a window a face that seems to belong to our gallery of intimate portraits; in a sleeping thoroughfare we hear a cry of agony and fear coming from an empty and shuttered house . . . at every corner handkerchiefs drop, fingers beckon, eyes besiege, and the lost, the lonely, the rapturous, the mysterious, the perilous, changing clues of adventure are slipped into our fingers. But few of us are willing to hold and follow them. . . . We pass on; and some day we come, at the end of a very dull life, to reflect that our romance has been a pallid thing of a marriage or two, a satin rosette kept in a safe-deposit drawer, and a lifelong feud with a steam radiator. . . .'

Many of O. Henry's stories are, in fact, the result of such nocturnal adventuring: nothing appealed to him more than to set a course after nightfall towards downtown New York, where in unfashionable streets and tenement blocks in the Bowery or over a two-cent coffee in some fly-blown café, some miniature drama, full of potentialities, might unfold; some dissolving view, as from a magic lantern, would set his imagination to work, or a hobo might pack a curious life history into the length of a cigarette. To O. Henry, the city seemed like a latter-day Baghdad, with himself as the Caliph Haroun al Raschid in quest of the adventure that lay round the corner. Dickens indulged in similar habits. Great deserted thoroughfares and narrow squalid courts appealed to him in the small hours, especially when revolving chapters in his mind; the rhythm of the body pacing through interminable darkened streets answers to the movement of the thoughts: night walking was a means of keeping his constitutional restlessness under control, besides offering possibilities of material. References to these night walks are scattered up and down his books, but the most complete are 'The Streets by

[9]

Night' in the *Sketches by Boz* and 'Night Walks' in *The Uncommercial Traveller*. They give a vivid picture of life in gas-lit Victorian London after dark, ending with a description of Covent Garden that seems the prototype of my own in this book, so little changed in essentials is the scene, even to the deadbeats and shabby coves of evasive aspect and malodorous presence who haunt the cafés.

These pieces of Dickens and the stories by O. Henry (albeit in New York) I look upon as primers for the student of nocturnal London—required reading for the amateur adventurer for whom this book is intended. The professional adventurers—the Marco Polos, the Columbuses, the North or South Pole men—are a bore ('half-adventurers', O. Henry calls them), for they have an object in view, they know where they are going, whereas the true adventurer—the amateur—never does. Chance is a fine thing, and he lets it make the running.

Always a restless sleeper, with an aversion to going to bed, my nocturnal journeys in London began when, as a university student, I had an attic at the top of a never-to-be forgotten boarding house in Endsleigh Street, Tavistock Square. Airless and close was that sky parlour, restricted its amenities and uncomfortable its bed. One night, as I tossed and turned, listening to the springs squeaking beneath me like a demented canary and endeavouring to stifle the noise of a jazzband across the street, I resolved to get to know the whole of London by night in all its aspects, and to commence my journeys forthwith.

It was 1945, and Tavistock Square was a wilderness of worn-out grass and shrubs. From the depths of the bushes came the gasps and giggles of the good-time girls, as American doughboys stuffed them brimful with their genes; farther on in Bloomsbury were cadgers singing or playing barrel organs in otherwise silent streets; end-of-the-world men were out in Tottenham Court Road; mock-auctioneers were still gulling simpletons and foreign servicemen in Oxford Street; whores idled about in platform-heeled shoes; an old man told me he was the rightful heir to a noble house, a title and a fortune out of which he had been sharked by the Government; and in Covent Garden a tramp broke a window in order to get a free night's lodging in the cooler. The entire perambulation had the ambiguous melancholy mood of Dr Johnson's poem, 'London':

> Here falling houses thunder on your head,
> And here a female atheist talks you dead.

It was a most satisfactory night, the trial balloon to countless other flights in which I extended my observations over the whole of Camden Town, Islington, Whitechapel, Limehouse and the Docks, as well as the Western and Southern areas and the late Victorian suburbs where Propriety and Respectability peer at the wanderer through the plaster alsatians of bay-windowed, Gothic houses down interminable streets.

For the space of a couple of hours, there is the restlessness that Dickens notes, as if the great city were having difficulty in getting off to sleep, but by midnight the feverish tossing and turning has subsided, especially in the City, where a silence unbelievable to those who know it only by day blankets the deserted streets. The only sounds are those of church clocks, the noises of the river (heard clearly in Spitalfields, as if only a stone's throw away), the cheeping of a disturbed sparrow and the footsteps of the policeman on the beat. The City and central areas are well lit (though almost entirely denuded of the rich effects the gas light gave), and you have leisure to study the buildings. One or two special areas, particularly Fleet Street, can hardly be said to settle down at all—there is always movement of some kind in the streets. The same applies to Smithfield, with the other markets, Billingsgate, Spitalfields and Covent Garden, returning to activity a little later, or a little earlier, on. There is always movement and interest at the big post offices, such as Mount Pleasant and the General Post Office, and no nocturnal adventurer worthy of his diploma will neglect a night or two at the great railway stations.

Waterloo is best in the early spring when the daffodils and anemones arrive in staggering quantities during the small hours from the Channel Islands. Paddington, when I lived in Marylebone, was a routine haunt of mine, for a never tarnished romantic view of the West of England mail trains, topped off by a wander down a selection of the dark and worn-out streets of this flavoursome quarter, where couples copulated in dingy, well proportioned doorways. Homelessness and hopelessness haunt Waterloo in these days, leaning desolately in cheerless corners or stretched on the benches of what is grandly termed 'the concourse'. The place is frequented by 'the woman in white'—a female dressed in white from head to foot, considerably less thrilling than the one in Wilkie Collins's novel; several vagrant women of the usual kind, loaded with bags, who make regular appearances on the benches of Victoria and Waterloo; and others not quite of this supposedly socially inadequate half-world, but on its fringe. The males include habitual drunks, cadgers, matchsellers and virtuosos of the tin whistle and mouth-organ.

Until a few years ago, Leicester Square was the West End address of many of these 'skippers' who have so sensibly, but uncomfortably, cut themselves loose from the strains and boredom of modern life. This site, under the gaze of Shakespeare, is now closed, but the Embankment and the Arches during the winter and the remaining bombed sites of Whitechapel and Stepney are still places which vagrants, unable or unwilling to go to a hostel, make for during the night. Sleeping rough is, however, on the increase, and the result is that these 'non-citizens', especially if solitaries, tend to spread themselves into fresh areas, such as Hammersmith. Again, night-walkers of professional status are to be found in Covent Garden—the young deadbeats and drug addicts, as well as the old, used-up

[11]

Striptease Lady
Soho

down-and-outs. Also on the move, and to be encountered at times, are the tramps and ex-mental hospital cases who pass through London by night.

Uncommon, hallucinatory experiences are also to be had in the Underground and other subways and particularly in the all-night conveniences. Young persons, hooked on drugs, giving themselves a fix, were common in the lavatories until notices announcing this to be a punishable offence appeared, and the junkies now have to go elsewhere to get high. A few years ago the addicts (I mean those who could get a legal fix) used to queue at all-night pharmacies, armed with doctors' prescriptions, fidgeting until their turn came. Having received their next day's quota, they would whip into the Underground lavatories to give themselves a dose of heroin or cocaine before the washrooms packed up for the night.

But strange sights can still be seen in some all-nite conveniences: those in my casebook include the middle-aged business man ('decent sort of chap, you'd hardly expect, Army-type, pity', said my friend, the attendant), who dressed himself in women's night attire from out of a carrier-bag—a vivid, silky affair, it was; the Frenchman who stabbed himself with a pair of scissors; and the old, well-dressed man who got undressed and went to sleep, quite naked, on the penny-house floor. . . .

*   *   *

'Our scene,' the cultivated voice from off-stage has in it traces of a Maryland accent (Maryland E., between Mile End and Plaistow), 'is a Japanese bride. She is to be bathed and perfumed by her illustrious master.'

We have left the non-citizens in their confusion and disorder, and, in the company of real citizens, are seeking strips with everything in Soho. Of course, we have become members of the club (annual subscription 5s.), and have got our cards to prove it. Before the lights go down and the girl appears in her kimono, we have time to note that our new club is open from noon to one a.m., or until two a.m. on Fridays and Saturdays. Our ticket of leave also entitles us to the facilities of other strip clubs—all with French or Latin-American names—and we note that members' concessions are valid only on production of our paid-up member's card.

What are these concessions? Not what you think, Big Brother. Striptease is respectable now; these places are decorous; a much applauded belly dance, perhaps a little discreet self-flagellation with the fly brush, but that's all. I tell you there's a complete absence of eroticism, although one or two *do* try—with a rope, or that bit with the toy bunny-rabbit, or simply by wiggling the bottom. Now and again you get a glimpse of pubic hair as the curtain falls; but otherwise, why, it's as harmless as 'The Follies of 1935' concert party on the dunes, when we got our shoes full of sand and they did those dramatic song-scenas like 'The Poisoned Cup' in old Cathay, though they still had their white plimsolls on. I tell you, you're behind the times, still in the Jack Spot Soho, when what Mr Butler saw was Vice and Iniquity, freebooting it in the streets.

In Sodom and Gomorrah they used to carry great big models of the male and female reproductive organs in public processions, to the sound of trumpets, and a low-minded lot they were. No wonder the Lord destroyed them. Well, there's none of that in Soho. There might be betting shops and beat clubs, strip clubs and dirty bookshops, drug taking and a bit of underground violence, but nothing objectionable, especially in the strip clubs. You could take your grandma.

While you've been distracting me, I've missed the Japanese bride. It's changed to Covent Garden . . . you mustn't miss this . . . Eliza Dolittle takes off everything she's got, except her straw boater. Of course, we can stay on to see it all through again. Lots of customers do. Some come two or three nights a week, and have the same seat. . . .

The clip joints can hardly be said to exist any more, but one or two carry on in a furtive, outlawed way. They were uniformly grubby and entirely boring. All that is needed to set up shop is a back room or cellar, a book for signing in the punters or clippies, odd tables and chairs and hostesses. You pay your fee (£3–£5) to talk to the hostess in the lonely hearts' club. You hope, and the clip joint owner hopes you will hope, to get more out of her than conversation. You pay ten

[13]

shillings for a near-beer (nothing more than shandy). You buy the girl a drink, more drinks. Her drinks have a cocktail stick in each, on which she gets five shillings a time. The dame leads the punter on to believe he will be able to take her home. He keeps on buying drinks as long as he can take it: her side of the business is to continue titillating him, and then cut out. Eventually he finds he's been gammoned or clipped, and that's where the trouble starts in this racket, where false pretences end in violence. Some aggrieved punters complain to the police, but others take matters into their own hands.

* * *

From clip joints to dirty bookshops—just the place to get rid of your blues in the night. Porn, near-dirty films and hot photographs can be bought very easily. There are over a dozen shops specialising in the erotic and kinky departments of literature in Soho alone. All are more or less alike—strip-lit, with a few hard-to-size-up characters turning over plastic-covered magazines inside, and a shop-window full of girlie magazines, books on sex and aberrations, Frank Harris's Autobiography, Kraft-Ebing and so forth, all comparatively tame. The real porn, the hard-core stuff, is for the back-room boys, starting at about four quid a time, but with part-exchange concessions. Photographs are done up in sealed packets. Ordinary sexual relations are classified as 'straight' and flagellation as 'flag'; but there are numerous other categories—homosexuality, lesbianism, bondage and rubber objects. The dirty books are usually typewritten and duplicated, of unknown origin and of the grossest obscenity, but there are more expensive Continental importations at an average price of £10, usually on flagellation or torture. Porn merchants make a comfortable living, with the rewards in the region of £10 a night for an assistant, while the manager of the porn-exchange can expect to make a clear £100 a week. Raids by the police are a professional hazard in this branch of literature, but so resilient are these shops, so well organised their supplies and so mysterious the real owners that they continue to flourish. After a protracted study of these establishments, my own conclusion is that they and their customers are insufferably boring, seedy and pathetic, at the same time adding a pleasing touch of drabness to London's night-life.

* * *

A decade on from the beat-music—coffee-bar era, when the discovery of Tommy Steele and Cliff Richard took the lid off a swarm of other (and usually considerably less talented) pop culture idols—here today and gone tomorrow most of them, the Soho coffee-bars seem to be living on in the afterglow of a lively, if edgy, period, on their memories of a brash teenage that spawned a new pop star every day and had its memorial in *Expresso Bongo*. Today, though new popsters

Southampton Strand
leading to Savoy
& Moore's
pharmacy in
Savoy Court.

One of a pair—the
other advertises the
Savoy Theatre.

continue to appear, the idols have ceased to be discovered in Soho—it's all over now and as dated as granny's photo album. London is like that: it takes things up—ideas, men and women, rock and rollers, pop showbiz culture, hipsters, outré clothes—with an intensity at times almost savage, sucks them dry and moves on. Today's in-people by tomorrow will become as old-hat as the spivs of the 1940s or the rubber plants, concealed lighting and bum-hole furniture of the 1950s are at present. This phenomenal power of absorption is by no means a new characteristic of London: it was the same in the 'nineties, when London was well aware that the Beardsley period was a bubble too fragile to last.

The 'nineties were, in fact, when London after dark was at its apogee. What we in these degenerate days have to enjoy is merely a fag-end—the stick of a burnt-out, splendid rocket. Yet, at times, in the great hotels and restaurants, at Drury Lane or Covent Garden, at a reception at the Mansion House or a dinner at Guildhall or the hall of a Livery Company, or perhaps especially on some festive

[15]

occasion at a West End club when the gas flambeaux are lit, we find that memorials of departed glories are still with us, recording a vanished civilisation, like the statues on Easter Island.

No part of midnight London has changed more completely than Piccadilly. At the turn of the century, the restless, nervous, garish circus contained within its perimeter the quintessence of London night life—the throngs of sightseers on the pavements, the horse-buses and hansoms, the flower girls and novelty sellers, the fashionable returning home from the opera or theatre, the Piccadilly Johnnies propping up the bar of the 'Cri', the exquisites lounging in the cigar divans, the top hats and opera cloaks, the newsboys calling, the tramps.

In the East End, only the down-and-outs and coffee stalls (the latter being a very characteristic feature of London's night-life for about 150 years) remain unchanged. The midnight stalls selling hot beverages, cheap meat, baked potatoes and shellfish have vanished from the Whitechapel Road, gin palaces have gone and the pubs close early, embargoed by the prohibitions of a dull and stupid age. In those days, the pubs offered a temporary escape from the horror of passing

time. Now the amusement arcades, offering coffee or Pepsi, do the same job. Endlessly changing imprints from a million feet make a pattern on the greasy pavement. Outside the night is dark and freezingly cold, but inside, in the Piccadilly playland (or the Crystal Room in the Strand, where the chandeliers give a top-notch Barbary Coast flavour to one-armed banditry, or in any West End nickleodeon or amusement arcade) everything is bright. Everything is all right in the slot-machine paradise. In the entrance by Scott's former restaurant, a young man, one of London's young drifters with his sleeping-bag on his back, is squatting Buddha-like on his haunches, buttering slices of Lyons bread from a bag, oblivious of the playboys and Twiggy-like playgirls. The clicking of the games is like the noise of a Brummagem factory, for the Tooty-Fruity machines are working overtime, and so are the Spinna-Winna, the Touchdown and the Big Time pintables. Indians, withered old men and women, deadbeats, smart guys, all with dead-pan faces, bend over the machines, wooing the fickle goddess Fortuna.

An old woman turns to me and observes, 'I hope there's nothing wrong with this machine, deary. Everything's wrong today. I lost my keys down the bog; this weather brings on my rheumatics. I'm eighty, deary. You wouldn't think it, would you now? I don't hold with the dezzimal coinage nor the Royal Family neither. We're the old ones, who don't count. Why look, I've won two bob. Two bob! I'm not going to lose it. You know the Man in the Moon at the World's End, deary? Well, I'm a-going to flog this bloody two bob on 'im. Expect I'll be back on the machinery tomorrow—it passes the time away.'

As I walk out a youngster says to his Twiggy, 'If you hadn't got green eyes, I wouldn't want to know you. That's the way I feel.'

* * *

Few of the great restaurants that gave richness and vitality to the London of half-a-century ago, as well as ministering to its gastronomic pleasures, remain. Dull nowadays at midnight as a county town, Piccadilly seems to have no hope left now that Scott's restaurant has departed, though the *coup de grâce* will be the building of the new and supposedly exciting Piccadilly, when Eros will become a memorial not only to Lord Shaftesbury but also to the extinction of interest. New restaurants, full of in-people and TV celebrities, are the thing now: the Trattoria Terrazza, L'Epicure, the Gay Hussar, Robert Carrier's in Islington, and the rest. Estimable though they be, I yet cling to my old favourites like Bertorelli's and Rules, and try to wish myself back into the naughty 'nineties in the former Domino Room of the Café Royal. Sometimes, as I wander round Soho at night and contemplate its transient pleasures and built-in obsolescence, I think I must be the only one alive to remember the Free French at the Café Bleu and at the York Minster on Bastille night: *Tempus edax rerum* is a fit motto for the parish.

[17]

Many of the old-fashioned restaurants and night-clubs showed a declension in numbers and in the will to survive about 1950: The Trocadero, the Holborn Restaurant, the Monico, Romano's and Frascati's were among the number that gave up the struggle for existence. About that time, I was sitting in Lyons Old Vienna and thinking of Albert Sandler playing in the big restaurant adjoining during the war, when the manager came up to me and told me it was on its way out.

'Why,' I said, 'there was no place I liked better than this in the blackout. I loved these eating boxes and gold-and-white decoration. One might agree that the apple strudel was a bit wartime, the Viennese pastries a little yellow round the gills and the mock cream a shade too mocking for some people's tastes, but I liked it better than the real cream we get now . . . and maybe the gypsy violinists *did* come from Worcester Park. . . .'

'Anyway, it's going,' the manager firmly replied. 'It's out of date. Old Vienna's had it. It's going to be cleared out, rebuilt entirely, and opened as a new, up-to-the-minute, quick restaurant, the Haversnack.'

Once again, *tempus edax rerum.*

There was a mildly exotic time—in the late Victorian age, throughout the Edwardian period and up to the 1930s—when London had all that ever approached a genuine Bohemia, with certain well-defined haunts as a background: the Café Royal, the Criterion and the St James's from the days of Wilde, Beardsley and Dowson up to about 1925; the Gaiety Theatre in the Earl-and-girl period of the Edwardian age; and various literary and artistic clubs such as the Savage, the Eccentrics, the Garrick and the Chelsea Arts Club, with a number of resorts in the shape of smaller restaurants, such as the Ivy, and various inexpensive cafés, for example the Dieppe and the Moorish Café, in Soho, and, of course, the pubs. There never was a Latin quarter in London: it was a myth, like the dissoluteness of Soho. The nearest London ever had to it was Chelsea, until the district became too expensive to live in, and the artists elected to beat a retreat to Islington, Camden Town and the purlieus of the Euston Road. Before the 1930s, the Bohemian and well-to-do layers were geologically separated. The struggling artists and their mistresses dined economically in Soho, and the smarties went to Ciro's, Murray's, the Ambassador and similar dining and dance clubs. When the wealthy got to slumming it in cheap Soho cafés, where supper cost three-bob including a carafe of wine, and tasting the joys of coffee stalls after a late-night dance, it was no use keeping up appearances: Bohemian London was on its way out, like Old Vienna of happy memory. Today London, which at that bygone period could hardly be said to go to bed at all, except in the suburbs, goes to bed early, and a genuine Bohemian, if he could be conceived as existing, would pass unnoticed among the crowd of hipsters.

* * *

How silent the City is tonight, and how dark and oily the river! I have been walking from the East End along miles of silent streets, under the shadows of gaunt and darkened warehouses, where the only signs of life are on the river— the constant patrolling of the Thames Police launches; the ships slipping down the river on a full tide, moving patches of darkness against the wharves, but partly outlined by the port and starboard lights and those on deck; and the lights of Limehouse Power Station. Had I turned North to the Commercial Road, I would have found more entertainment, for there lorry drivers gather in cheap caffs that remain open long after the rest of the East End (apart from the restless citizens of Skid Row) has closed down for the night. Here tarts of supremely unattractive aspect, that one would surely not touch with the proverbial barge pole, prowl up and down on the pavement in search of clients, and down-and-outers, who have cadged a cuppa from an easy-going lorry driver, stay in the warmth as long as they can spin things out or until, becoming a nuisance, they get the bum's rush. On this evening, however, I have continued on by the river

[19]

shore through Wapping to Tower Hill, where one or two lights burn in small windows here and there in the Tower, though that ancient fortress, as brooding and mysterious as the river itself by night, has put its shutters up long ago with that strangely moving institution acted out each night over past ages, the Ceremony of the Keys.

Apart from the Post Office and hints of life at the fire stations, the City is absolutely empty east of St Paul's. The great banks and offices recall nothing so forcibly as the monoliths of some lost civilisation; and the churches, temples of a vanished religion—which, indeed, in this infidel age, they all too often are. Waste paper is being blown about the streets in an arbitrary movement, both melancholy and dispiriting: one wonders whether this aspect of London after dark is even more discouraging than that opposite one of synthetic joys among the playboys in Bunnyland in the exclusive gambling clubs. Only the collections of waste material outside shops and cafés, a stalking cat or a copper on the beat indicate any kind of life, until Fleet Street is reached. The Embankment is almost deserted, but the river, oily black, catching the starlight on its waves, is at its most memorable and beautiful. The arches and the rusticated masonry of King's College are like an effect by Piranesi, though made tender by shadows cast by the waving branches of the plane trees, and the sense of solitude is somewhat modified by warm and

friendly lights from the *Discovery*, the *Chrysanthemum* and other ships moored in King's Reach.

The Silver Lady, who dispenses nocturnal charity in the shape of a slice of bread, a cup of tea and a fag to sundry ragged men and women about town on the Embankment, has departed for the night, leaving behind a residuum of shadowy vagrants, one of whom joins me as I contemplate the sable river and asks me if the Silver Lady will be open tonight—the opening gambit of a touch! As this fails, he tries with a hard luck story—how he somehow failed to get on to things in London, how, as a result, he has walked that day from Kent, meeting with nothing but snares and delusions by the way. Unfortunately, I have heard it all before, for he told it to me once in St Dunstan's-in-the-West, and his spiel forms one of the fugitive histories in the casebook I have collected on the underworld of London, whose prophets write their messages on lavatory and subway walls. I shake him off, for a more interesting appointment awaits me in Carmelite Street, by certain newspaper gratings, where I seek audience of a super-tramp who resides there, one who has been on the telly and briefly in a film, and is thus a Vagabond King.

*   *   *

Villiers Street, as Big Ben strikes three, is a dead loss. There is nothing to be seen but the dustbins. Even the birth-control shops are shut up, and tonight the Arches are deserted. Yet I hear the strains of a violin: there is an old, old man, playing to himself—or to no one—in a wind-swept door: a perfect subject for a mad modern play. I pass on uphill, pondering, not for the first time, on the absolute meaninglessness of life. The Strand is brilliant, the watering cart having passed that way, and the smooth, petrol-sprayed surface of the road reflects long lines of dazzling electric lights in iridiscent waving ribbons of prismatic colour, like the Aurora Borealis. Apart from newspaper vans and cabs, the street is deserted, but a few starlings squabble on cornices, and a solitary pigeon plods along hopefully.

But in the alleys off St Martin's Lane and on the edge of Covent Garden are white-faced, immobilised, adolescent drug addicts, homeless, sick and frowsy, of both sexes. Many of these derelicts come on to the streets by way of the innumerable beat clubs, where drug pedlars are a regular part of life, like encyclopedia salesmen in the suburbs. These clubs often change names and premises as fast as the police catch up with them. Low-class clubs of this sort—grubby, back-alley, down-the-cellar-stairs—proliferate in the Soho area. Each is like the other as far as my experience goes: it was my intention to include a drawing of one of these scruffy dives—a collection of half-baked heads and shaking limbs, gyrating in the foetid air to the sound of amplified pop—but the only way to record these joints adequately is on film. Meanwhile, the underground routes of amphetamine drugs and cocaine and heroin flourish in the concrete and asphalt jungle of Soho, and

[21]

the white-faced, dithering derelicts prop themselves up against the walls of Covent Garden. Visits to the streets of the area, to St Anne's Court in Soho and the all-nite coffee clubs of Wardour Mews, also in Soho, are required subjects for all who aspire to graduate in the knowledge of London night-life.

The list of the more presentable as well as lively and entertaining clubs for the under-twenties is almost endless. Unfortunately, many of these clubs have a short existence. A built-in obsolescence that any progressive manufacturer of consumer goods might envy restricts their span of life on this planet; and some simply go broke. This uncertainty of tenure makes a working list impossible to compile. Hence the value of the so-called underground press—*The International Times* and *Oz*—which youngsters read for news of the clubs and to keep themselves generally on the scene. At the time of writing, such clubs as the Middle Earth (Psychedelic, Indian dances), the Bag of Nails (Discotheque—music, drinks, food, somewhat smarter), the Speakeasy (Chelsea types, well-dressed hippies) and the Roaring 20s (coloured members, West Indian and beat music) can be cited as representative samples of this off-beat explosion of clubs. Perhaps the greatest curiosity among them, apart from the U.F.O. at Chalk Farm (the strange world of Arthur Brown, and various freakish happenings, impromptus with a view to revolutionary visual effect), is the King's Hovel at King's Cross, a Methodist night-club open until 2 a.m., offering beat and folk music and food in an atmosphere considerably more healthy than that usually encountered in Soho dives.

In general, London seems to be gradually regaining somewhat of the late-night interest it had by all accounts in the Victorian age—in degree, though not in kind. In fact it is considerably more interesting from the point of view of the nocturnal wanderer than the French capital. In recent years, I have spent a number of nights prowling round Paris from dusk until daybreak, finding much less free entertainment than I had anticipated—apart from Notre Dame, the Cité and the Seine at midnight and the twinkling lights of Paris from the heights of Montmartre —when the last foolish tourist has gone delightedly home, the last café has closed and Madame is counting out her money. Never failing in interest by day, the quays and great boulevards are incredibly monotonous and lifeless by night— I mean in the small hours—and, in this aspect, London is infinitely more fruitful both of nocturnal happenings and of fine arrangements of light and shadow on architecture. Therefore, I unhesitatingly advocate the joys of night wandering in London, and suggest to those of its *aficiónados* who have not yet tasted them to do so without delay—equipped with sandwiches, tobacco and thermos, to turn night into day—seeing in the dark like many of our four-footed friends who decline to go to bed with the sun. . . .

Back to obscurity, then, to friendly, all-enveloping Night, to midnight skies, to subtle, inconclusive adventures in great thoroughfares and dingy back streets!

[22]

The Drawings

1

Royal Opera House, Covent Garden

THE LONDON SEASON—an all but moribund institution, though once thought as inevitable a part of London life as the rising and setting of the sun himself— reached its apogee in the Elysian 'nineties, when it constellated round the persons of the Prince and Princess of Wales. It began with the Boat Race and progressed through the Royal Academy Private View Day, through Ascot and Henley, innumerable garden parties and drawing-rooms (here we cannot but think of Lady Bracknell) and a first-night at 'the Garden' to end on the lawns at Goodwood. After which, the great patrician families and their imitators went out of town, and dust-sheets shrouded the salons of Grosvenor Square.

Curiously enough, out of the wreckage of the past, a first night at the Royal Opera House has still something of a special quality about it, an éclat that seems proof against this reach-me-down age. The theatre, built by E. M. Barry after the fire which destroyed Smirke's 1809 Opera House in March 1856, has a rich yet discreet interior—one which has often solaced me when, bored by Puccini or Schoenberg, I have longed for the cigarette interval in the crush bar. The building will hold an audience of some two-thousand people, yet twenty minutes after the final curtain it is almost deserted. To watch the well-heeled audience emerge—the fur-coated (and sometimes opera-cloaked), rich middle-aged stepping into their chauffeur-driven limousines and the leggy young girls chattering nonsense to their stylish escorts as they head for Chelsea or Hampstead—is truly entertaining, especially when, as occasionally happens, the stream of fashionables is joined by a bit of floating jetsam in the shape of a wandering down-and-out making for a kip in a corner among the cabbage nets: at first glance as off-key as a Jarrow marcher in *The Bystander*, but, on a second, we become aware that he has fulfilled his destiny and added the one touch that was lacking in a fundamentally Victorian composition.

2

The Post Office Tower from Charlotte Place

THE POST OFFICE TOWER, uncomfortably like the Tower of Babel in Breughel's picture of that name, is essentially something to be seen at night, like all the recent commercial architecture of London. By day it dominates too many vistas, often quite unexpectedly, making the great city contract optically by reducing the apparent distance between areas in which it is a landmark. At close range it has had the unfortunate effect of dwarfing the neighbouring terraces and turning shabbiness by juxtaposition, into positive decay.

My illustration was made from the corner of Rathbone Street and Charlotte Place, where the contrast between old and new is very marked. Explore the area by night, as Sickert used to. There is an old-fashioned dairy, an old-fashioned barber's, an old-fashioned dining-rooms with mirrors and bentwood chairs and a tiny florist's shop, the headquarters of Miss Katie Kent, for fifty years flower seller outside the Middlesex Hospital—and all in Charlotte Place. As I progressed with my drawing, admiring the orange lights from the window of the Duke of York and sustained by the smell of kebab from a Greek café, a woman came up to inform me that the tower was already historic, because it was the place where Jeremy Thorpe, the Liberal leader, proposed marriage. . . .

RATHBO
STREET
LATE
BENNET
STREET

Post Office Tower
from Charlotte Place

Geoffrey Fletcher

3

Rupert Street Market

THE MARKET in Rupert Street, like that of Berwick Street, where Jessie Matthews' father kept a stall, is best seen in an autumn or winter dusk, for the architecture in each street (Berwick Street is separated from Rupert Street by Brewer Street and a narrow passage lined with sexperiences) is of no particular account: the interest is in the brilliant colour of the fruit, flower and poultry stalls under the electric lamps. Rupert Street, however, has some shops worth study—the Hong Kong emporium, the basket shop and one or two others with Victorian façades around which the goods are displayed—and these add to the interest of the scene.

Rupert Street was magnificent before the war, for then the stalls were lit by hissing, flaring naphtha lamps, the market kept going till a late hour and the poulterers and butchers specialised in cheap, knock-me-down offers. In those days, you could get a rabbit for a shilling or less: thrifty Londoners would make for the market to buy a cheap weekend joint at the last minute. Fruit and flowers are the main commodities nowadays, but Rupert Street has a bookstall—one of the few literary depots (if not the only one) in Soho where you can buy books on subjects other than sex. As a proof of this, I have encountered authors of such unquestionable probity as Arthur Mee, Bishop Butler, Dr Samuel Smiles and Mr J. B. Priestley: nothing could be more impeccable than *them*.

4

Chestnuts up West

CHESTNUTS, and hamburgers to boot, under the soft orange light from the windows of the pub and the blinding electric light provided by the Westminster City Council in Gt Windmill Street.

Says the chestnut man: 'Put me in your drawing, and I'll give you a load of nuts. I've always wanted to go in a book.'

These I decline. Later comes a creature that I take to be a youth, wearing dyed flaxen hair, dark specs and a suit seemingly run up out of his grandmother's cretonne curtains. This apparition also wants to go in the drawing: pathetic, when you think of it, this widespread desire to be recorded. Only the old news-vendor at the corner remains stoically indifferent to immortalisation, no doubt because of the fugitive, impermanent nature of his wares—violent death, the collapse of empires, assassination and suicide in cheap hotels.

My acquaintance with this corner of London goes back to the war, when I used to frequent a long-vanished establishment on the opposite corner called the Rainbow Room. Americans occupied the pavements in those days, and they still do, as rubber-necked, naïve and self-assured as ever. The St James Tavern with its Alhambra-like door, strange mouldings and fine sandblasted glass is really more interesting from the outside than from within, in common with many Victorian pubs which the brewers have not actually spoiled by wholesale remodelling but have dimmed or watered down by flock wallpapers, chandeliers and such-like intrusions. Easily accessible London pubs worth seeing by night from outside include: the Museum Tavern, opposite the British Museum, the Final in William IV Street near Charing Cross Hospital, the Paxton's Head, near Knightsbridge Green, and the Camden Head, Camden Passage, Islington (see page 101). Interiors worth visiting by night include the Red Lion, Duke Street, St James's, the Crown, Aberdeen Place, St John's Wood, and the Salisbury, St Martin's Lane (illustration on page 65).

5

Fleet Street, winter evening,
rush hour

FIVE O'CLOCK in Fleet Street on a winter's evening and the rush hour beginning to build up. A full moon hangs low over the City in a soft, velvety, grey-blue sky, and below it is the floodlit St Paul's, bisected by the spire of St Martin's, Ludgate, all solid black, a spear triumphantly brandished. Blurs of red and yellow light are the buses, blurs also of yellow light are the trains incessantly rumbling across the viaduct. The crowds push in both directions, their faces strongly illuminated as they pass the display windows of the newspaper offices. One realises why Dr Johnson was so attached to Fleet Street and the justice of his famous encomium on it: though still a village street in a certain sense, it has a vigorous life and vitality entirely its own, unobtainable elsewhere. Even in the small hours, Fleet Street is less deserted than other thoroughfares, for, apart from those recognisable as being concerned with the production of newspapers—Fleet Street's village craft—there is a succession of well-dressed, City-type men carrying umbrellas or briefcases nearly always to be seen sauntering leisurely in the direction of Temple Bar and stopping now and again to window-gaze. This proceeding at two or three o'clock in the morning is one of the mysteries of London. Besides these, there is usually a gathering of otiose characters, either in Mick's all-nite café or perambulating the pavements.

Geoffrey Richards
Fleet Street, Winter evening
rush hour

6

Jazz at the Old Place, Gerrard Street

THE CELLAR in Gerrard Street (*on* Gerrard Street, if you are really hep) where Ronnie Scott began was perhaps the most interesting of the jazz caves in London, and a good spot, too, for members to drop in for refreshment, liquid or solid, whether you like experimental jazz or whether, like myself, you believe all the best jazz, like all the best architecture and all the best books, came into being some time back. It may be that jazz (unlike pop, which is sterile) is developing but, if so, the growing pains are somewhat alarming. The cellar, drifting with smoke, was full of young people, sitting at the tables, drinking beer or coffee and listening attentively and sympathetically to the musicians, for they took their live jazz seriously at the Old Place.

The cellar had a welcoming atmosphere; older, squarer types merged easily into the environment, instead of sticking out, as elsewhere, like prehistoric monuments. The jazz, screaming, angry, disintegrating or tragic by turns, was largely improvisation on saxophone, bass, piano or drums, with tremolo solos that belonged to the Devil's own confessional. The bass sobbed out its anguish as the sweating, close-cropped coloured boy beat the daylight out of it, and trumpet and saxophone, fearful of melting, cried out for release, like souls in Purgatory. At intervals, when you least expected it, a sizzling chord took off from out of the band, like a Minuteman rocket, sometimes successfully (this being followed by a round of applause), at other times to burn itself out harmlessly, hissing in a corner.

It was a loss to London's night life when the Old Place closed. Ronnie Scott's other club, somewhat less casual, in Frith Street remains as a compensation. There, for a modest membership fee, one can wine or dine until three o'clock in the morning to the accompaniment of some of the best jazz in London.

Jazz session at
The OldPlace
Gerrard Street

7

Albert Bridge, Chelsea

ONE OF THE most charming prospects in London was the view of Albert Bridge with festoons of coloured lights—not overdone—outlining the girders seen through the trees from the large window of the Blue Cockatoo, a country-town restaurant in Chelsea, demolished in 1967 and ever to be regretted. This was best arranged on an evening in early autumn, before the leaves had fallen, or on a summer night. The view can still be got from the street, though less satisfactorily, for no window frames the composition.

The drawing opposite shows the bridge on a grey November evening, without the electric lights but with the illumination from the splendid original gas lamps—sufficient with the spots of light on barges or from the windows of the warehouses and the dark reflections in the shining water to create a perfect example of that Chelsea riverside poetry which Whistler and Walter Greaves made peculiarly their own. The Albert Suspension Bridge was designed by R. M. Ordish and opened in 1873 and, with its original gas lamps and toll houses still intact, belongs to the Chelsea of the great period—the age of Carlyle, Rossetti, Whistler, Greaves and Wilde. The bridge is somewhat in the style of the Gothic revival of the eighteenth century—the Walpole period—combined with a lightness and elegance that the Victorians usually reserved for the cast-iron architecture of their new seaside resorts.

Albert Bridge

8

Fleet Street: the light in the West

THIS VIEW of Fleet Street, with the tower of St Dunstan's and part of the Law Courts with its illuminated bracket clock, set against the fading light of a winter afternoon, was painted in the 1880s, more or less from the same position, by Atkinson Grimshaw, until a few years ago an unduly neglected Victorian painter. His work has now returned to favour, and rightly, because he had a true feeling for the poetry of architecture—particularly that of city streets at twilight—unusual among topographical artists. Today the evening rush has replaced the evening hush, the hansoms and horse-buses have departed and, of the several decorative hanging lamps prominent in Grimshaw's painting, only those of El Vino's and the Cheshire Cheese survive.

The tower of St Dunstan's-in-the-West, one of the most satisfactory designs of the Gothic revival, belongs to the early 1830s, when the church was rebuilt by John Shaw. This truly romantic tower, a sort of miniature Fonthill, seen under conditions of mist and sunset, lifts this aspect of Fleet Street decidedly out of the commonplace.

9

Printing the Daily Telegraph

I HAVE CHOSEN this subject to represent the many industrial activities (if a news-paper is an industrial product) that take place in London in the dead of night, simply because there is something strange and romantic about the production of a great newspaper that only the most case-hardened Fleet Street cynic can gainsay, though the days when writers like Sir Philip Gibbs could call Fleet Street 'the Street of Ink' and write novels about journalists and their sob-sisters and get away with it have gone for good, fortunately.

Three outstanding characteristics mark the printing of a newspaper: the noise when the machines are running (contrasted with the near-silence of Fleet Street); the hurried efficiency of the printers (each man knowing his job and doing it); and the novelty, an almost eerie novelty to those unaccustomed to it, of reading tomorrow's news the night before. The *Daily Telegraph* has seventeen high-speed rotary printing presses in the machine-room; the number of units run will depend on the size of the paper. There are five units to each machine, and each unit can produce eight pages, making a forty-page paper. On the extreme left of the drawing is one of the conveyor belts which take up the supply of printed and folded copies from the presses to the publishing room, where they are bundled, labelled and despatched to the vans waiting to transport them to the railway stations.

The *Daily Telegraph* uses an average of two-thousand miles of paper each day, the Continental copies on light-weight paper forming part of the first edition, with an airmail edition on airmail paper. The first edition is printed between 10 and 10.30 p.m., the second between 11.30 p.m. and midnight, the third between 12.45 a.m. and 1.15 a.m., and so on until 4 a.m. By then, the most perishable of all commodities, today's news ('a history of the world, written, printed and distributed during the twenty-four hours it covers'—the *Daily Telegraph*'s own definition of a newspaper, which cannot be bettered), is on its way. Soon it will be time to write the palimpsest over again. . . .

Printing the Daily Telegraph

10

Coin-op all-nite launderette

LAUNDERETTES or washerterias, providing (at least in the East End) subjects that would have appealed to Steinlen for his lithographs, have established themselves rapidly as a characteristic part of London's night-life in all districts. Ultimately they may rival the Abbey, the Horse Guards and the Tower of London as indispensable items on the vacationist's itinerary. These neon-lit, coin-op establishments all possess a basic feature in common—the customers sitting it out, each watching the bubbling, sudsy scene through the porthole of his or her particular Bendix in a hybrid atmosphere combining that of a doctor's surgery with the suspense of a turf accountant's, the whole laced with the flavour of a whiter-than-white TV ad and memories of the old time bagwash.

Apart from these fundamentals, all-nite launderettes or washerterias vary subtly according to the area; those in Hampstead and Chelsea, for example, are distinctly high-toned, one in Hampstead actually having mural decorations. Their clients vary too, so that someone washing his underpants for a private whim in a distant part of town can be readily singled out as a displaced person. Small cigars are smoked to while away the swirling, lathery vigil in Hampstead, and bottles of *vin ordinaire* are not uncommon. The man with the beard and duffle-coat seen through the door of this East-End all-niter belongs to the far West—Kensington or Chelsea. I took him for a paperback writer, drumming up copy; he turned out to be an educated, progressive alcoholic, seeking identity on Skid Row. Or at least that is what he told me.

11

The Empress, Brixton

THE SOUTH LONDON CROWD going into the Empress, Brixton—'the home of the pro's', as it used to be called by music-hall artistes—can be contrasted with the West End crowd coming out of Covent Garden, although West End music-hall fanciers find their way to Brixton whenever the theatre presents a suitable bill. There is a notable absence of limousines in Brixton, and a notable presence of cloth caps. . . .

It was at the old Brixton theatre, predecessor to the present one, that Gertie Gitana and G. H. Elliott decided to form their own company, but the most historic of Brixton's music-hall nights began with the opening of Don Ross's 'Thanks for the Memory' at the Empress in April 1948, a record-breaking show of old-timers that appeared at the Royal Variety Performance at the London Palladium in November 1948 and, after touring the country, returned to the Empress for its final performance on December 2nd 1950, when Gertie Gitana announced her retirement from the stage. Lew Lake had a show starring Wilkie Bard, Vesta Victoria, Fred Barnes and Harry Champion at the Empress as late as the 1930s. There were giants in the land, even in those days. But music-hall nights belong to the dead past of London, as incomprehensible to the young as a Sunday School outing, and to them every bit as fusty.

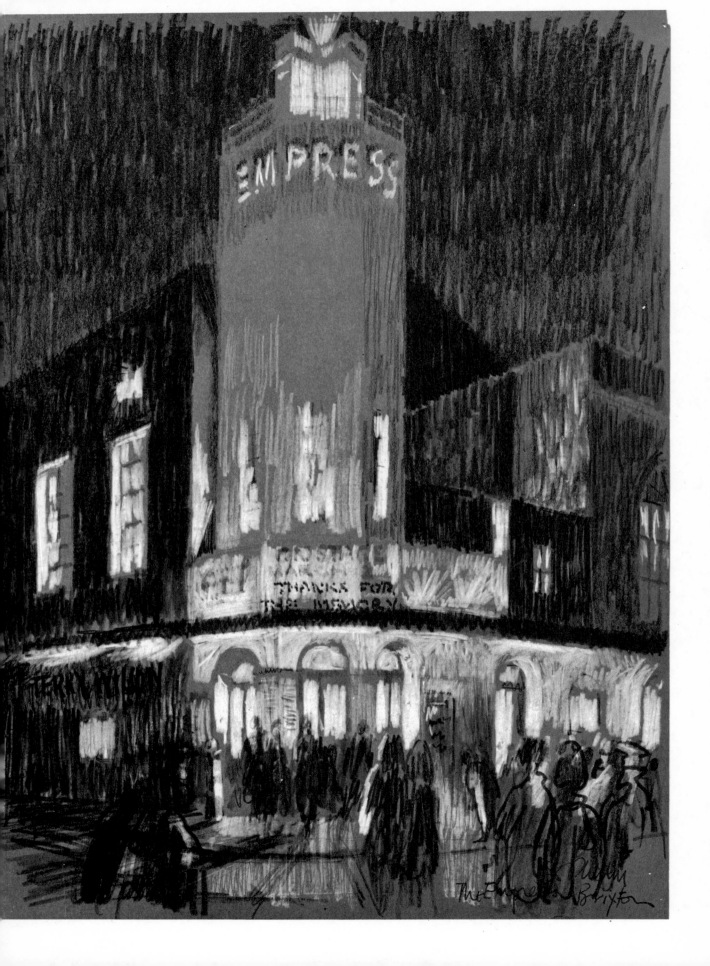

EMPRESS

12

Saturday night at the Biograph

IT WAS a question whether I chose to illustrate a night at the Players or one at the Bio as an example of the choice specialist entertainments—I refer to those beyond reproach—in London at night. Most of the others, though strongly flavoured to suit a palate as coarse as mine, are unsuitable for pictorial treatment from several points of view. . . . I chose the Bio for its authenticity and rich period flavour.

It is with a pensiveness amounting to positive gloom that I realise I am old enough to have held on to my seat at the Perils of Pauline (Lord, how those actors had to work in those days!) though admittedly the Perils were of a respectable age by then and were scratched enough to have been under a glacier. Still, the consolation is that those days—the Harold Lloyd–Chaplinese era—were the golden age of the cinema, practically everything else since being a bore, with the excitement and delight clean gone out of it. Regrettably, old films are not the regular fare at the Bio, except when it celebrates yet another jubilee. The Biograph, the first cinema to be built as such in England, dates from 1905. The interior, the projection box and the egg and dart mouldings are original; the exterior has recently been revamped and spoiled. The cheap seats are also, I imagine, original; tip-up, of wood and of an uncommon firmness, they appeal only to the bottoms of pensioners. Men appear to form the greater part of the audience: some bring their food with them, and consume it even during the big scenes.

Going to the Bio is a long-established tradition in Pimlico, but, besides locals, the cinema has *aficiónados* like myself who come from farther afield: there is even one who flies over regularly from Paris. There is an agreeable feeling of lethargy among some of the pensioners, though they will, when the occasion demands, rouse themselves from their stupor to address a few remarks to the lone stranger on the screen or to the dreadful character who has come out of the twenty-first century, forgetful that they are, like themselves, but walking shadows. I rate the Bio as one of the most interesting experiences to be had in London, and Saturday night is the best time to experiment. So, if you want to re-live your past, go west, elderly gentleman: take a ticket to Pimlico and an evening in Vauxhall!

13

Covent Garden, 5 a.m.

DAYBREAK on a raw January morning and the fruit and vegetable markets of Covent Garden rapidly building up to their busiest time of day. Endless oaths, endless rumbling of lorries, endless rumbling of barrows loaded with onions, cabbages, carrots, plants and boxes of fruit, and shoved by long lines of porters working like coolies, crossing and recrossing, in and out of the avenues of the market hall. Here, a load of cabbages turns the corner too quickly, collides with another and bursts over the paving stones: the four letter words which form the comments of the porters seem to pass unnoticed by the nun who is trundling her own barrow of greens off the scene. There, at the corner of Henrietta Street, one of the two coffee stalls of the Garden is working overtime, dispensing cups of tea and coffee to the gentle sound of frying eggs and bacon: 'Two teas, Fred . . .' 'Cup o' tea, Bill—hot next time.' The deadbeats and junkies have faded with the first streak of light in the east. After their departure come the buyers from the big stores and the restaurant proprietors, filtering in among the milk deliverymen, the piles of vegetables and the concentrations of chugging lorries.

The flower market, entered suddenly from the dark, cold streets, is unbelievable: a true temple of Flora, fragrant with the scents and made delightful by the colours of spring. There are the daffodils that come before the swallow dares, jonquils and anemones, all in boxes open for the inspection of the trade, iris, roses, pots of plants and orchids. Sparrows are starting to cheep in the girders. other sparrows answer them from the cornices of buildings outside. The steely blue sky is becoming paler and diffused with a soft, peach-coloured light under the banks of indigo cloud. Early risers, well-dressed men and women, are appearing in town once more. A homeless woman who has slept in the Garden all night, with a net of cabbages for a pillow, picks up her bundle of possessions and shuffles into the shadows. . . . Another London day is beginning.

Covent Garden
5am S.S. Ruskin

14

A voice crying in Leicester Square

SUNDAY comes, and with it, on a hot evening in Leicester Square, the religious cranks and hot-gospellers, holding banners aloft, each with his curious shiny vestment painted with verses from Scripture. In fact, *all* the pounders are out in force, among the swarming crowd of provincial vacationers, bullet-headed Americans, junkies, nut cases, foreigners, strange youths wearing *art nouveau* print dresses, whether male, female or borderline, and bewildered elderly couples. You can feel the air on your skin—vitiated, dust-dry, cotton-woolly, the plane trees droop in it. Long-haired youths try to flog drawings, distantly resembling London views; Indian brassware men are importunate, and so are the flower-sellers, the newsvendors, the postcardmen: the smell of booze mingles with the smell of sweat.

Among the crowds, the banner with the strange device is held by the original absent-minded professor. Fellow hot-gospellers are busy unpacking handouts from a motorised tabernacle parked on the west side of the square.

'If I were as ignorant as you,' says the end-of-the-world man. 'I'd get someone to educate me—to teach me to read. I'll show you the way to Heaven.'

A face in the crowd says, 'Show me the way to go home'—a witty sally that gets a big laugh from the listless, perspiring group by the lavatories.

When the laugh has gone the rounds of the rubbernecks, the latter-day evangelist adds: 'I'll tell you why you won't be converted. It's because you like Sin.'

A girl says: 'I must hand it to them, getting up and saying all that. I couldn't do it, not reely.'

By now, reinforcements of gospellers have turned up, but the crowd is already falling out to seek fresh amusement elsewhere. . . . What think ye of Christ?

15

The Palace of Westminster

A ROYAL PALACE has stood in Westminster, between the Abbey and the river, for close on a thousand years. The fire of 1834 destroyed all the ancient buildings except Westminster Hall and the cloisters and crypt of St Stephen's Chapel. The foundation-stone of the present building by Pugin and Barry was laid in 1840. Other designs submitted in the competition for the new Palace of Westminster can be seen in the Jewel Tower. By the time the work was finished, the perpendicular style chosen to harmonise it with the Henry VII Chapel was no longer fashionable; the Gothic revival had moved on to other styles which would undoubtedly have proved less satisfactory had the rebuilding occurred later.

The view of it from across the river in Lambeth is one of much grandeur, especially by night. Floodlighting suits the architecture admirably, softening the monotony of the repetitive panelling, throwing parts into deep shadow and blending well with the honey-coloured stone. Crowds in summer dress stroll on the Embankment below the hospital, enjoying the view, the night air and the musical sound of the softly lapping river, the waters of which—of a lilac several shades darker than the sky—reflect the orange-coloured lights from the windows of the great Gothic building. As the light fades, the river façade takes on the appearance of a golden casket. Next, the western mass containing the Victoria Tower is switched on—this portion previously being in dark-blue shadow—and the effect changes again to become one of the romantic, fairy-like palaces that Victor Hugo imagined in his drawings.

16

Destitute woman, Westminster

IN CONTRAST to the illuminated splendours of the Houses of Parliament, this drawing is of a destitute woman on a doorstep, also in Westminster, though it could be any street in London in the small hours of the morning. The vast majority of rough sleepers are men, but women are taking to this way of life in increasing numbers. Few are drug takers or methylated spirit drinkers, and they differ again from the men in being almost always solitary and given to carting their few belongings about, with quantities of old newspapers and cardboard for bedding, in decrepit old bags. If you haven't got a home, it's an offence to sleep in public places, God knows why.

Most of the homeless women I have spoken to range from the mildly eccentric to the distinctly dotty, with the occurrence sometimes of the high-grade mental deficient: the last, of course, is an official terminology, not mine, for my notions about what constitutes mental deficiency are by no means clear-cut. What is certain is that they are often undernourished or verminous or both.

Homeless women—they must be destitute—are sometimes accommodated in the government reception centre in Gt Guildford Street, Southwark, formerly a debtors' prison, but there are women's hostels, mostly used by regulars, with beds at four-shillings-and-sixpence a night. None the less, many prefer sleeping rough to doss houses and institutions, except in the winter. It's all right in the summertime, when the nights are warm and short, even though the lavatories are locked up and you have to go in the bushes. The most difficult ones are the lesbians. For them, either under the Arches or under one of the bridges on the Embankment is the most welcome kip. Elsewhere they are the most unwelcome of all the misfits.

Destitute woman
Westminster

17

Muriel and Nosher at the Colony Room Club

THERE MUST BE more clubs in Soho than in any other square-mile on earth: beat clubs, foreign clubs, jazz clubs, social clubs, jean-age clubs, drinking clubs, coffee clubs, hostess-with-the-mostest and hostess-with-the-leastest clubs: there are whip clubs, clip clubs, non-stop strip clubs: Sally clubs, pally clubs and dirty back-alley clubs. Soho has the lot as part of the traditional bill of fare it has been offering since the 1760s when Mrs Cornelys opened Carlisle House as a place for assemblies, masquerades and other more dubious entertainments—the first of a flush of midnight queens that more or less died out with Kate ('Ma') Meyrick, doyenne of night-club proprietors, best remembered for her '43' Club in Gerrard Street, but promoter of a dozen others—Dalton's, the Folies Bergère, the Manhattan and the rest. All had the same simple money-making idea: round-the-clock drinking in the company of pretty girls, one that paid dividends in the Roaring Twenties. Clubs are like plays—they have a long or a short run; they either catch on or people lose interest in them and they just go broke.

Muriel Belcher's twenty-year-old Colony Room Club, with Ian Board behind the bar and Nosher to keep an eye on things, is today perhaps the best known, as it is certainly among the best run, private drinking clubs in Soho. In the Millionaire's Diary, the members are listed as including royalty, peers of the realm, top writers, painters and film executives. Actually, the members are far more interesting than this seems to suggest. In fact, I am myself on the books, membership of the Colony Room being more or less essential if you want the low-down on what's going on in Soho or even if you just want a comfortable easy place to drop in for a drink. The atmosphere is that of a successful party, where the people get on with each other, where things are said that are worth saying and where bores are not. . . . Nosher must be the best informed dog in London, and could make his fortune as a columnist any day.

Muriel S Nosher
G S Philbin~ Colony Club Sho

18

Provocative ladies, Soho

EVEN THE MOST unobservant traveller in Soho parish cannot fail to notice the number of girls hurrying along its streets, with skirts and eyelashes reaching towards the heavens and carrying small cases. These are the strippers of Soho's brave nude world, en route to the next striptease club. A good stripper can earn up to £200 a week: most, as far as my extensive observations go, have not enough character to be good whores, or even bad ones, let alone make a career on the stage. In the age of mini-skirts, stripping is not what it used to be. Most of the girls are scantily clothed to start with, and this blunts the point: a fan dance singularly fails to excite when you've seen everything there is to see before it starts.

The shows vary from the somewhat puritanical to the definitely randy; the smarter they are, the less erotic, as a general rule. The stage is small, and the strippers, therefore, dominate the audience (no doubt intentionally) which is invariably middle aged male, with an occasional coloured man or oriental thrown in for flavour.

In this club, the atmosphere is decorous, and the joint is run with assembly-line efficiency. The pattern of each 'act' is, first, music followed by a brief announcement; more music; next the posing in clothes (sometimes while the stripper mimes the words of a song); and then the inevitable perfunctory removal of clothes under changing effects of light. There's a strange lack of eroticism, though one or two try with a rope, a luminous toy dog or simply by wriggling the bottom; then comes the polite applause as the stripper raises her hand to show her pubic hair (between crossed legs) as the curtain falls. The man in the front row returns to his evening paper. He is, I guess, the most obsessional newspaper reader in London, and a gift to its publicity department.

Provocative Ladies Soho
S P Fletcher

19

The Red Mill Club, Macclesfield Street

BESIDES the Red Mill Club in Macclesfield Street, there is also a Moulin Rouge elsewhere in Soho: you pays your money and takes your choice. You pay your £1: why not spend the whole day, and bring sandwiches? For the man outside offers a non-stop live show, and this is fair enough: once you are a member and have paid for the show, you can sit there for hours, watching an endless succession of acts, each with its little props, including mildly erotic efforts, such as the Jamaican girl on the previous page with the naughty rope between her legs, to the tune of 'This is my Seventh Letter'—the most sexy turn of the lot. ('Nice girl,' said the man in the paybox. 'Good figure, knows her stuff. But you'll have to see the other coloured girl.')

Eventually, in nearly all these clubs, incredible boredom sets in. The complete lack of viciousness gets on one's nerves. At the Sunset Strip in St Anne's Court, there are even Victorian ballads between the acts. Everything is *comme il faut*. There are, of course, really randy striptease shows, grubby and back alley, if you plumb the depths of Soho, but for the most part the nuderamas are very respectable. No reason why a suburban husband should come home with the old extra-work-at-the-office chestnut: nowadays he can excuse himself with, 'Thought I'd have a quiet evening at the strip club'.

Many members turn up regularly enough to make these 'clubs' something more than a polite fiction. Some of the girls are on a five club circuit, from noon to midnight or later. Once their 'act' is over, they are off, clattering past the audience carrying their little bags with their costumes in them. It's probably Janice's or Miranda's or Samantha's turn next. . . .

20

Sex films, day and night :
St Anne's Court

ST ANNE'S COURT has a razzmatazz atmosphere entirely its own, especially by night. You feel it as soon as you step in there. You can let your hair down good and proper. For instance, there's dirty books, the most porny ones being in the inner sanctum sanctorum. The customers are so dull that you can hardly believe they are so depraved as you would like to imagine, as they silently inspect the plastic covered books classified under leather (or rubber) garments, bondage, flagellation—all stimulating and bizarre. There's the Sunset Strip, where the customers are nearly all regulars and where plenty of good chicks are to be seen, including Miss Rosie with her little Gay Paree act in front of the Eiffel Tower. An old, disintegrating man comes up to me, and says I ought to be saved—that though my sins be as scarlet, they shall be as wool.

Another kinky happening occurs when a prostitute or tom hails me from a staircase with her cheery 'Hello chum. . . .' By day, there are no nameplates to be seen in St Anne's Court, but, after dark, they mysteriously appear round the doors: Miss Bettina, Miss Lola, Miss Gina, all sexy fatale, all French models. If you have blues in the night, ring and walk up.

At the sex cinema, they charge £1 for admission. For this, whether the Soho cadet likes it or not, he only gets sexy films. 'You know,' said the young man at the door, 'pretty randy, but not blue, definitely not blue.' These films are imported from Denmark and Sweden. But the real thing can be had elsewhere at £4 a time, a showing which includes the milder one-pounders thrown in—Lesbian films 'and things of that sort'. These films are made in Soho. Of course, the blue-film world includes racketeers who would entice a punter (or simpleton) in on a £5 ticket and then do a bunk without showing him his films. These operators are a nuisance to the genuine blue film men.

21

Interior, the Salisbury

A SPRINKLING of beards and moustaches, plenty of 'darlings' in the conversation, magnificent vistas of mirrors, marble and mahogany, a rich smoke-filled atmosphere and you have the Salisbury, St Martin's Lane, one of the two finest late-Victorian pubs in the West End. The patrons are largely actors and their camp followers, with a few cranks, tourists and refugees from the twentieth-century like myself added for variety. It provides after dark one of the few authentic *fin de siècle* experiences remaining in London, either inside sitting at the tables in the plush-lined boxes with the superb *art nouveau* statues of Diana, which serve as electroliers above, or standing at the elaborate bar watching the reflections of pillars, heads and lamps in the decorative mirrors, or else simply standing outside in St Martin's Lane admiring the effect of the light through the etched glass of the windows.

Though the food is good and the place well run and lively, it is this special gas-lit quality of the naughty 'nineties which makes the pub so satisfactory. The Communist Party, nastiest of all political parties (and that's saying a good deal), used to meet in the upstairs room of the Salisbury, prior to 1939—about the only worthwhile thing, I suppose, they ever did.

Geoff Fletcher
The Salisbury

22

Chez Victor

THE CHEZ VICTOR in Wardour Street is notable in these days for making no concession to flashy décor or up-to-the-minute gimmicks. Like the Restaurant Maurer in Greek Street, it's always the same. The interior is dark and lined with mirrors. There is a vintage ladies and a vintage gents up the lino-covered stairs, a coloured lithograph of Janville, 1870, on the landing, and an album, which Victor will produce on demand, with autographs of all the stage celebrities, mostly in insanely bad handwriting. 'No, we don't want to cheenge,' says Madame. 'Ze customers, they don' want to cheenge. Last year, we cheenge lino an' ze customers zay we don' want dese cheenges. . . . Ah, yees, monsieur, eet eez like a bistro, a bistro à Paris. We don' tart it up, yees? Eet's been like thees for sixty-seven years.'

There are bottles with candle-drips on the tables under the Lincrusta ceiling, all, like the mirrors and their endless reflections, part of the turn-of-the-century atmosphere. A table in the window is the most agreeable position in which to dine at the Chez Victor, for this enables you to watch the shadowy figures in the street beyond the curtains, not only those that pass in the night, but also those that slip furtively into the welcoming, brightly-lit birth-control shop opposite, and these birth-controllers are an admirable background, in my opinion, to Tripes à la Mode de Caen.

Chez Victor

23

Great Windmill Street

THOUGH the Windmill girls have departed and a cinema and gaming club have taken their place as the chief entertainments of the street—if you except the handful of strip clubs and one or two other rum joints in the precinct—Windmill Street after dark is still its old, edgy, synthetic self. It is worth a quarter-of-an-hour of anyone's time merely to savour the Coney Island atmosphere or simply to study the desolate tourists, the rich nut cases and the hipsters and freaks with which the street abounds.

The Nosh Bar in Great Windmill Street must have been visited by nearly everyone of note or otherwise during the last twenty years. Its salt-beef sandwiches, with, of course, a dish of gherkins, are second to none: as good as Bloom's, Whitechapel, I believe. You will perhaps hear the proprietor's brother informing a customer that the Queen's equerry drops in for a sandwich; or you might encounter that worthy yourself. If distinguished customers fail to show up, you are still left with the satisfaction of eating at one of the earliest, and probably the best, snack-bars in Soho.

'We never closed' is still a good motto for Great Windmill Street, the nearest approximation to the Montmartre flavour London offers. Besides the flashing lights and country cousins, are a plentiful supply of leather clothes and the shortest skirts in town.

24

Piccadilly

PICCADILLY and Saturday night go together, especially in the tourist season, when a thousand cameras click under the winking signs. Piccadilly is vulgar, brash and awful, and it ought to be left alone: the planners, with their redevelopment schemes for rationalised transport, pedestrian-circulating areas, and the rest of the familiar crap, by which a largely ignorant and powerless public is conned, will, of course, ruin it.

On a Saturday night the flower-sellers are in full bloom, as are the novelty vendors, the snack-bars and the sellers of badges and postcards. Lord Kitchener's Valet seems larger and noisier than ever before: it is arranged like the old-time bazaar, but the goods are strictly up-to-date or beyond. They include reprints of posters, badges, Union Jack clocks and gents lavatory notices, all sold by floosies displaying equally generous quantities of eyelashes and legs. Deafened by the noise, bewildered by the glare, his entire frame reeling from the assault, an old, old man staggers out into the crowds, clutching a bag of sweets; pigeons and long-haired youths drink at the fountain; a mesmerized, middle-aged couple from the provinces find themselves in Vanity Fair.

In the small hours, Piccadilly is disappointing. There are only one or two drug addicts to be seen nowadays—you hardly ever find them having a fix in the lavatories—though there are rough sleepers, sometimes, on the prowl at week-ends, after Thursday's National Assistance pay-off. The advertising sign over the 'Cri' appeals to no-one but the Westminster Council's dustmen, as they come to empty Piccadilly dustbins and to sweep up the hamburger bags and newspapers. But by five there are already new newspapers coming on the streets: a few early birds are buying them from the man on the pitch opposite the Café Royal.

25

Leicester Square : the old Soft Shoe

THERE IS no room at the Chicken Inn: a view through its windows discloses a perspective of chewing faces. Outside, a crowd of idlers gathers to watch Jumping Jack, first Earl of Mustard, perform his dance routine to tape-recorded music on the pavement. His Lordship is accompanied by his personal man, whose offices include the holding of his master's fur coat, which Jack takes off at intervals when he gets too hot, at which times he fans himself with his hat.

The Earl of Mustard, who appears in my James Mason film, *The London Nobody Knows*, was once on the music-hall stage. He can now make £3 on a good evening, and likes nothing better than adding to his collection of eighteenth-century-style clothes. Once I caught up with him when he was doing a little mild advertising in Fleet Street, pushing an old bassinette on behalf of an antique shop: many an earl has done worse things for money.

On another corner of Leicester Square, the neon-lit figure of a fraulein (Nelly the Barmaid?) winks in and out, inviting you to drink the best German beer and dance to your heart's content at the Wunder Bar below. Hot-dog men push across the foreground, seedy gents endeavour to disburden themselves of revolutionary pamphlets, dead-beats spring up from the greasy pavement like unsavoury weeds, and Asiatics leer longingly at girls' legs. . . . The furtive, flashy qualities of Leicester Square are developing rapidly in the night air.

26

The last troubadour

ONE-MAN BANDS are a rarity in London these days, and I consider myself fortunate in finding one for this book, to represent the vast army of theatre-queue performers unknown by name or rank who for generations past have entertained the crowds for early doors—paper tearers, Shakespearean reciters, tumblers, musicians, at one time as essential a feature of London by night as its very gas lamps and now, like them, a vanishing race: *sic transit gloria mundi*. A business man singled himself out of the crowd of playboys, playgirls and galleryites, and asked me why he, the troubadour, didn't get a proper job of work. I replied that (1) a proper job of work was an indefinite article, open to a variety of interpretations, (2) it was none of my business, nor yet of his, and (3) he was working at being young, at living for the moment—not at all a bad thing.

Afterwards it struck me that the remark about working at being young opened up fresh, unusual and attractive possibilities—if only one knew how to stay young. If only one knew what youth was, for that matter, much less how to use it; but you never do until it has gone for good. If only one had the courage to chuck the lot up, to take to the streets with a one-man band and become the last troubadour!

The Last Troubadour

27

Down and out on the steps of the Lyric, Hammersmith

A WET NOVEMBER NIGHT in Hammersmith; six o'clock by the Guinness clock at the Broadway. Already a castaway, one of the thousands who sleep rough in London, has kipped down for the night on the steps of this disused theatre, which has the most exquisite auditorium in London—not that he cares. The more fortunate ones—the voucher men—will sleep in doss-houses like the Salvation Army Hostel in Great Peter Street, Westminster, or in places such as the St Giles's Centre, Camberwell. They are the élite among the vagrants. The subways are lined with damp humanity, each unit intent on getting back to its establishment in a more delectable suburb: Hammersmith, cold, wet and late-Victorian, has no charms for them. Buses circling round the Broadway are a blur of red and gold— a little out of harmony with the drab surroundings. Still, there is a welcome glow on the wet pavement from Lyons, from the big Victorian pubs (from the Hop Poles especially—a Victorian pub at its most excellent best) and from the market stalls. Two boys claim a penny for the guy, a figure wearing a pair of old Welling-ton boots and a faraway, glazed expression. An old woman wearing a cloth cap passes—a survivor of nineteenth-century Hammersmith—shambling along to the jug and bottle in the old style.

Much later that evening, I return from my night tour of Hammersmith, when the crowds have gone, when the caffs have their chairs upturned on their tables, and when the only noise is that of a flossie giggling down an alley. The man from nowhere is still there, indifferent to the rain, sleeping on the steps by the market place at the eleventh hour.

28

Cheyne Walk

IF YOU WANT TO KNOW why people who can afford it live in Cheyne Walk and its immediate neighbourhood, go down there on a moonlit evening. You will find a special atmosphere, one that remains inviolate in spite of the Blackpool Illuminations-like lamps, an atmosphere unique in London and about the only genuine artistic thing left in Chelsea.

There is a party on at Don Saltero's, No. 18, once the coffee-house cum museum of curiosities kept by James Salter, 'Don Saltero', later a public-house with a huge lamp outside and charmingly drawn by Walter Greaves. Variously gorgeous, well-got-up females arrive with their escorts, one of whom wears an opera cloak, giving a curious feeling of the 1920s to the scene, when Chelsea artists and their models frequented the now vanished Blue Cockatoo. Chelsea is fine after dark. When I lived there, I used to spend entire nights mooning up and down Cheyne Walk and the little squares, studying the effects of light made by the gas lamps, as they were then, and thinking of the Queen's House (the one with the big iron gates) and the dreamy, long-necked Rossetti women who came there, the back garden full of strange animals and Rossetti, himself, strangest animal of all, bearded, saturnine, infinitely gifted and maddening.

There is a long haul between a top notch, Cheyne Walk at home and Sam's motorised, gaslit hot-dog stall in Chelsea Manor Street, but Sam still makes one of the best cuppas in London.

Cheyne Walk

29

Holly Bush Steps, Hampstead

HAMPSTEAD, like the small squares of Chelsea, is particularly attractive after dark, once the evening rush-hour traffic has thinned out, though here again the replacement of gas light by more modern forms of illumination has considerably reduced the quality of the effect of light and darkness on its small eighteenth-century houses and old walls. Nevertheless, Holly Bush Steps, with Golden Yard to the left, remains a choice backwater, even without the pussies in boots. At the top, the lights of the Holly Bush beckon through its decorative windows. The interior of the inn, wonderfully untouched, is no anti-climax; there are wainscoted screens, a grained bar counter and splendid old glass advertisements for Benskin's Ales and for Hooper's Original Brighton Seltzer from the Royal German Spa, Brighton, and with these goes an interesting collection of faded Victorian photographs. When George Romney's studio next door became the Assembly Rooms after his death, the landlord of the Holly Bush did the catering for the élite of Hampstead. In essentials, the inn has changed little since the time of Dr Johnson and Boswell, who were among its clientèle.

Another Hampstead evening effect worth mentioning is the view from a point half way down Flask Walk, looking back towards the lighted windows of the Flask Tavern, with the little old-fashioned mixed business on the left, before they put up their shutters for the night. There is also the splendid panoramic view of London from the windows of Jack Straw's Castle.

Jolly Bush Steps —
with pussies in boots

Hampstead.

30

Goldilocks and the two bears,
Blackheath Fair

LONDON'S FAIRS are best seen at night, for the kindly darkness softens hard edges and the signs of wear and tear, not least on the human elements. Electric bulbs on the outside of the walk-up show illuminate a painting of a blonde pursued by a lion and a cohort of ignoble savages. She wears tights and an ample bra: the question is, what was she doing in the jungle? Anyway, she turns her eyes up to Heaven, as might be expected, awaiting a sign. Inside, both human and animal life are distinctly less exciting. The animals are caged, and the lion visibly bored with the whole outfit. Moreover, the bears, muzzled, are only harmless honey-bears—Goldilocks may throw away her spear.

Vacant youths, palpably less intelligent than the collection of animals behind them, stare and comment on the girl's figure, as if she were a waxwork or a prize sow. Her sister is in showbiz too. She is in the booth next door, billed as the Egyptian princess, covered all over in gold and asleep for two thousand years. . . .

31

The Discovery *and the King's Reach*

FIVE O'CLOCK on a winter evening. The sky in the west is fading from amethyst to a dull, smoky orange, barred at the horizon—that is, over the pinnacled and turreted flats farther along the Embankment—by bands of indigo and grey. There are lovers dawdling and homeward-bound City types walking briskly under the trees. The buses over Waterloo Bridge look like metal toys. The remaining leaves on the plane trees show as shrivelled patches of dull browns and olives in the lamplight. Beyond the bridge, the floodlit tower of Shell Mex House, resembling some ancient gigantic mausoleum, makes a long path of reflected orange in the water, orange over blue and, nearer, orange over grey. As the light fades, the hideous shape of Waterloo Bridge is absorbed into the distance. The flag comes down from the stern of the *Discovery*, and, in the darkness, ducks appear on the water, tiny specks of life among the chains in the shadows of the hulls below the massive granite walls, bobbing on the waves made by a passing ship, apparently unconcerned.

In the small hours, the Embankment is comparatively deserted in the winter, even by the vagrants, though there are more people about than one would suppose. Even the Streatham-bound buses have a fair number of passengers. Then the dark, oily water is brilliant with moving silver reflections from the lights on Waterloo Bridge and the moonlight or starlight reflected on the waves of a full tide.

The Discovery
King's Reach

32

4 a.m., Covent Garden: music for the junkies

THERE is more light, and there are now more people on the London streets in the early hours of the morning than ever before—too many people, in fact, for complete enjoyment. Covent Garden, which used to be deserted until the lorries arrived, is now like a setting for *The Beggars Opera*. A colony of junkies, drop-outs and non-citizens has established itself, and music of a melancholy character is usually provided for them, either by some young busker with a guitar or by the Irish character ('Oirish Guards in the Great War, bandsman') with the accordion. The Welfare Officer of St Martin-in-the-Fields is on duty all night: if the deadbeats want to commit suicide, they ring him up. They hang about as if waiting for a firing squad. From time to time, the junkies disappear down the lavatory steps to give themselves a jab.

As the day breaks and the lorries arrive, the hippies, vagrants and drop-outs gradually disappear. Many set a course for St Martin's Church, where they drape themselves about the steps, waiting for the crypt to open about 9 a.m. You can see them, of both sexes, all young, incredibly desiccated, often bare-footed, far gone in drugs, leaning in a stupor against the church walls. Soup is provided for them on Sundays.

33

Underneath the Arches

THE ARCHES, less popular with rough sleepers these days, is yet a locality well worth visiting after dark, if only to enjoy Craven Passage, with its old-fashioned grocer's and wine merchant's, the fine early nineteenth-century façade of the Ship and Shovel and the light coming through its decorative, sand-blasted glass windows. Note, by the way, the words 'Public Department' on the middle doors. I have read of a scheme to turn the Arches into a passage of small shops, yclept boutiques: this, of course, would entirely destroy its character.

The Arches can usually be relied on to produce some odd situation or character after nightfall. There was a solitary pavement artist as I made the drawing. He exhibited two specimens of his handiwork, each in a frame of white chalk, like a plastic doyley. One was titled 'The Last Mile Home', a white caterpillar road bending to the horizon under a blue sky and a lonesome pine, and the other was 'The River', again with a solitary tree, this time a dead one, and long sunset reflections under a poached-egg sky.

34

St Pancras

THIS, perhaps the most splendid Victorian Gothic building in London (and certainly the masterpiece of its architect, Sir Gilbert Scott), has in recent years begun to make friends and influence people. Once, like the Albert Memorial, it was a type of all that was then supposed to be preposterous, meretricious and escapist in the Victorian age. Now there is every hope that the building will be preserved, though this, of course, is not enough: it ought to be cleared of all its modern accretions, equipped with contemporary engines and carriages, buffet, news-stands and slot machines: then, gas-lit once again and staffed with porters in corduroys, it should be run as a pure Victorian experience. The station hotel, still with many of its original fittings, ought to be re-opened, complete with chambermaids in lace caps and streamers.

This truly romantic building, a cathedral to the Victorian god of steam, is a marvellous spectacle at any time of the day. But see it when the westering sun has gone down over the far end of the Euston Road and the last light has faded on its towers and spires; when the traffic below is a blur of red and gold, and the station a dark, mysterious silhouette, indigo-blue against a background of purplish greys; when beetle-like figures, hurrying home along the pavements to the suburbs in a winter dusk, add a drab, Welfare State touch as a counterpoint to a Victorian harmony that might otherwise be too painful to be experienced.

35

Castles in the air:
the Regent Street lights

IT IS early in December, and there are dense crowds along the pavements of Regent Street, up from the suburbs, for the most part, but with a lacing of provincial and foreign visitors, too, all come to see the lights and to stare in the windows. It is easier to move on foot, for the traffic is at a standstill or, at best, just crawling along. There are family groups accompanied by their dogs, though it is hard to imagine what these, their four-footed retainers, see in it. There are hot-dogs, also—a stand on every corner along the street—and chestnut men. The woman balloon-vendor is doing a notable trade. Round the corner in Regent Place is a red van, and a man inside it blowing up more balloons. A couple of kids in relays rush further supplies to the woman. You can see these balloons, some with a snowman in them, others with fish, bobbing up and down the whole length of the street, under the white-and-gold lights and the suspended silver castles. Once in a while, one of these balloons takes off and floats up into the darkness to an unknown destination, and its bereaved, youthful owner weeps, or laughs: it all comes to the same.

The toysellers thrive in the shop entrances: 'Here you are, mechanical toys. Two bob cheaper than the shops. If they didn't work, I wouldn't sell 'em. Here you are, now, the crawling babby, the youngster that winds up, and the rolling po-leece man. All guaranteed, and only a few left.'

Regent Street
- Castles in the Air

36

Christmas tree in Trafalgar Square

MARTIN LUTHER is said to have been the first to take a fir-tree indoors, where he illuminated it in honour of the Nativity, an idea he got from seeing the stars above the trees during a walk in a fir-wood. The custom of having a Christmas tree in England is due to Queen Caroline of Brunswick and the Prince Consort. The most charming expression of this tradition is, perhaps, the annual gift of a superb tree from the City of Oslo to the City of Westminster. There is also a crib, bedecked with branches, harmless enough, one would think, though it created a disturbance among hypersensitive fools when introduced a few years back. Usually there are Norwegian choirgirls in national costume, various Father Christmases dotted around, and a military band that plays carols and popular classics before the Mayor of Westminster opens up. Flash-bulbs explode all over the show, as the cameras click. A great gasp goes up from the crowd when the lights go on, for its individual members are mostly middle-aged and middle-class, steady-goers who are unaccustomed to the idea of London's being switched on.

In all, the scene is one of the most attractive to be found in London after dark, especially if the weather has been seasonably cold, when icicles hang like giant combs from the bronze figures of the silent fountains and the stars in the London sky try to rival the single brilliant star the tree wears for its brief period of glory.

37

Christmas in Carnaby Street

EYES LIGHT UP when switched-on Christmas comes to Carnaby Street; not only the electric eyes slung across the street, but also the dollies' eyes, the ones with the yard-long lashes. Only the more with-it family groups appear here: running the gauntlet of the lights, the swinging shops and the scenesmen is too much of a traumatic experience for the middle-aged, mostly.

The dollies' eyes in the panels spanning the street have electric bulbs for pupils —orange, red, blue, green and yellow—and surrounding the heads are Union Jacks and small figures of Carnaby Street-like characters. There are also large stars at intervals, possibly to remind us that it's Christmas.

On the pavements are more coppers than I ever remember, even in this area, and from out of the crowd rise innumerable foreign accents, punctuated by transatlantic drawls. Old-young men, heavily bearded and wearing fur coats, prop up the bollards at the corner of Ganton Street, accompanied by their leather-clad, wellington-booted fun molls—interesting enough to the novice, but not quite so traffic-stopping to the seasoned student of way-out London, who has seen them all before. Has Carnaby Street, then, passed its apex, like all perishable things, and is it now on the downbeat? There are signs that it has. New shops with weeks of life in front of them consider it more fashionable to be out of Carnaby Street than in it, and I, backward glancing always, am already nostalgic about it and thinking of its golden age of a month or two ago.

38

New towers of London—Millbank

THESE new towers of London have little to recommend them except by night, when, on a reduced scale, they repeat the effect of the New York skyscrapers, forming crossword-like patterns of light in the darkness.

The Vickers tower at Millbank, besides being more stylish in the best sense than most of the others that disrupt the London panorama, has the advantage of having a riparian site, with the result that truly spectacular reflections from its lights occur on the ever-changing waters of the river. Other blocks, less well placed, have to rely on wet pavements for their fortuitous qualities. It is interesting, too, to watch the changing lights in these buildings themselves, as groups of windows or whole floors are switched on or off. A good murder film might be made out of this occurrence as a variant from the time-honoured sequences of chases across roof tops, girders or scaffolding.

39

Camden Passage

TIME WAS when Camden Passage, Islington, was a narrow dark alley lit by gas lamps projecting at eccentric angles, a place of small shops with a local trade. Today its antique shops, ever multiplying and ever more lush, illuminate the alley from end to end. It is a droll enough comment on changed times that the *objets d'art* on display are often of a kind once chucked out by the aboriginal inhabitants of the area. . . .

Drunken women are at a premium in the alley today, and dead-end kids, smelly and with a racking cough, are equally hard to come by. The alley cats, furtive and of doubtful lineage, have gone—or almost. Only the newsagents, the toyshops and the gramophone emporium remain from the bad old days. Even Lou's old clo' shop—the last relic of feudalism—has gone and its place has been taken by yet another café-bar. And the Camden Head—that peerless pub of authentic rococo opulence—has come out in a blaze of Blackpool-type lights, reminding me of that illuminated tramcar of old time, with the dubious word 'Progress' written in electric bulbs. . . .

CAMDEN HEAD

CAMDEN
PASSAGE

Camden Passage, Islington

40

Pub window

DECORATIVE embossed windows, perhaps the most characteristic feature of the nineteenth-century pub, itself a descendant of the gin palace, still beckon the thirsty the gregarious, the communicative and the down-in-the-mouth ones across the darkened London landscape, just as they did to the Victorians, to whom such windows blazed a warm gas-lit invitation to escape momentarily from life in the bottom drawer: for the lush Victorian pub, full of mirror and mahogany, brass and mosaic, was and is the ultimate in escapism from the pressures of urban life.

The windows are often superb examples of a craftsmanship in plate glass now almost entirely defunct. Floral and bird designs in a more or less rococo framework, reproduced by means of deep cutting, embossing and acid etching, are general motifs. These windows at the Camden Head, in which birds' nests, marigolds, convolvulus and roses are combined with scroll and curlicue decoration and fishtail half-Gothic lettering, are especially fine examples of the genre.